INTRO

ALWAYS BE WILLING AND OPEN TO LEARNING NEW RECIPES AND TRYING NEW CONCEPTS.

-DREUX ANTOINE

FROM THE AUTHOR

As a young boy growing up in New Orleans, I grew up around culinary professionals including my double great aunt Helen DeJean founder/owner of Howard's Eatery which she opened in 1932 and later opened the world famous Chez Helene Restaurant in New Orleans. My aunt Helen spent most of her time pouring into her nieces and nephews which created great home cooks like my grandmother Joyce DeJean and my cousin world-renowned culinary pioneer Chef Austin Leslie. I remember as a young boy watching my family work at my great aunt's New Orleans famed restaurant Chez Helene everyday and the amount of hard work associated with owning and operating a restaurant. I believe my drive and passion came from watching them labor for so many years. I didn't understand that this was the learning grounds and beginning for me and would ignite and help me discover my passion for "Culinary Life".

I want to dedicate this project to my great aunt Helen DeJean, my great-grandfather Sidney DeJean, my grandmother Joyce DeJean, my mom Belinda Johnson and my cousin world renowned culinary artist Chef Austin Leslie. They helped me discover my "Inner Chef" and helped me turn my "Purpose into my Passion".

FROM MY KITCHEN TO YOURS

The 'Soulful Chef Cookbook Volume 1 is first of 10 cookbooks in this series designed to help teach, guide and inspire individuals. My hope is to bring families back together again in the kitchen and at the kitchen table. This cookbook features meals that will nourish the mind, body, soul and spirit of the family.

This cookbook is a step-by-step guide designed to help individuals prepare some of today's popular cuisines with a little added "Soul". You will learn how to prepare meals for your family and most importantly for you to enjoy preparing meals at home with your family.

This cookbook series will introduce and present to you cuisines and concepts in the following categories:

American
Asian
Creole
Creole-Soul
Latin-American
Mexican-Amercian
Italian
Soul-Food
World Cuisines

KITCHEN ESSENTIALS

In order to fully understand some of the basics of the kitchen let's discuss some key cooking terms and techniques to help prepare some of your favorite meals.

MIREPOIX

A mirepoix is diced vegetables including carrots, white onions and celery cooked for a long time on a gentle heat without color or browning, usually with butter or other fat or oil. It is not sautéed or otherwise hard cooked, the intention being caramelized for added flavors. The "Mirepoix Technique" is used for soups, gravies, toppings and garnishes, and many sauces.

"Roux Mirepoix"- consist of diced bell peppers, green onion, white or yellow onion, celery and garlic which is used for famous dishes including Gumbo, Gravies, Rice Dishes, Soups and much more.

5 MOTHER SAUCES

Béchamel- A roux whisked with dairy to make a white sauce.

Velouté- A roux whisked with chicken, turkey, fish or any other clear stock. The resulting sauce takes on the flavor of the stock, and the name is derived from the French word for velvet meaning smooth and delicate.

Espagnole- A basic brown sauce. It's made of brown beef or veal stock, tomato puree, and browned mirepoix.

Tomato- This is made by cooking tomatoes down into a thick sauce but used to also be thickened with roux.

Hollandaise- This is the one mother sauce not thickened by a roux. Instead, it's thickened by an emulsion of egg yolk and melted butter.

ESSENTIAL TECHNIQUES

Sauteing- Pan-fried or Pan-Seared in oil or butter in direct heat
Grilling- Technique used to cook on a ridged heat source with Grill Marks
Broiling- Used to cook foods for charred flavor in high heat
Roasting- Form of "Surround-Heat" Cooking applying indirect heat
Poaching- Used to gently cook foods in a simmer submerged in liquid
Blanching- Saltwater brought to a boil and veggies are cooked briefly
Braising- Used as the "slow & low" technique to cook food for long periods
Frying- A method to "deep-fry" or "shallow-fry" breaded foods in fry oil
Baking- A method used to cook foods in the oven

THE
SUCCESSFUL
COOKING GUIDE
OF A CHEF

ಜಬ

Recipes & Techniques prepared by Dreux Antoine

Table of Contents

CHAPTER ONE

In this chapter we will cover 5 popular soups that are easy to make and will make your family love you forever. Maybe!!!

- Lentil Soup
- Tomato Basil Soup
- Chicken Noodle
- Vegetable Soup
- Seafood Gumbo

Lentil Soup Recipe

Recipe Serves 6-8 servings

INGREDIENTS:

Water
Lentils
Dry Basil Leaves
Diced Tomatoes (14.5 oz)
Chicken Base
Mirepoix
Salt
Black Pepper

Cooking Instructions

In a medium or large stock pot add 8 1/2 cups of water

Add 3 cups of Lentils

Add 2 tbsp of chicken base

Cover Lentils with lid

Bring Lentils to a boil and lower heat to med-hi temp

In a saute pan or skillet heat 1/4 cup of oil

Add 1 cup of each of mirepoix and allow mirepoix to caramelize

Once caramelized add mirepoix and liquid to Lentils and cook for 35-45 mins

Stir to make sure mirepoix is blended with Lentils

Constantly stir to keep Lentils from sticking

Add 1 can of diced tomatoes (14.5oz)

Add salt & pepper (season to taste)

Add 1 tbsp of basil leaves

Add 2 bay leaves (Keep Whole Do Not Break)

Add water as needed

Cook Lentils until they are soft; do not scorch or let Lentils break

Garnish with sprinkled basil leaves and scoop of goat cheese

Tomato-Basil Soup Recipe

Recipe Serves 6-8 servings

INGREDIENTS:

Diced Canned Tomatoes- 14.5 oz
Whole Tomatoes
Chicken Base
Heavy Whipping Cream
Diced Celery
Diced Yellow Onion
Minced Garlic
Salt
Black Pepper
Onion Powder
Garlic Powder
Dry Basil Leaves

Cooking Instructions

In a medium or large non-stick pot or pan add 1/4 cup of oil and heat at med-hi temp

Char-off 4 whole tomatoes cut in half and let char and soften/blackened

In a large stock pot add 2 quarts of heavy whipping cream & 2 cups of water and heat

Add charred tomatoes to pot of cream

Add 2 cans of 14.5 oz can of diced tomatoes and cook at med-low temp

In a separate saute pan add 1/4 cup of oil and heat

Add 1 cup of diced celery, yellow onion, minced garlic and caramelize (5-7mins)

Remove from heat and add to pot with heavy cream and charred tomatoes

Add 2 tbsp of chicken base (season to taste)

Add all dry seasoning (season to taste)

Stir and mix all ingredients well

Cover soup with lid and let cook for 25 minutes at med-lo temp

Lower heat to hand blend or remove from heat to blend in food processor

Hand blend soup with hand mixer or blend in food processor until smooth texture

(Transition blended soup back into pot if blended in Food Processor)

Constantly stir soup to mix all ingredients

Add water as needed

Season to taste

Serve in small bowls and top with roasted crutons

Homemade Chicken Noodle Recipe
Recipe Serves 6-8 servings

INGREDIENTS:

Pulled Chicken Breast
Chicken Base
Mirepoix
Salt
Black Pepper
Onion Powder
Garlic Powder
Chopped Parsley

Cooking Instructions

In large non-stick skillet heat up 1/4 oil to saute 2lbs of diced chicken breast for 7mins
(Pulled chicken meat can be substituted as well)
Season with a pinch of McCormick's Grilled Chicken Seasoning

In a medium or large stock pot add 10 cups of chicken broth & 4 cups of water
Add 1 tbsp of chicken base and whisk into liquid and bring to a boil
Add mirepoix
Bring liquid broth to a rolling boil
Reduce heat to med-low and add chicken meat
Add dry seasoning (season to taste)
Constantly stir soup to mix all ingredients thoroughly

Cook Linguine Pasta (OPTIONAL)------> Follow Package Instructions
(KEEP SEPARATE/ON THE SIDE DO NOT ADD TO COOKED SOUP)

Vegetable Soup Recipe

Recipe Serves 6-8 servings

INGREDIENTS:

Diced Canned Tomatoes (Drained)
Chicken Base
Corn Niblets (Drained)
Okra
Large Diced Mirepoix
Chopped Cabbage
Cut Green Onion
Diced Green Bell Pepper
Parsley
Salt
Black Pepper
Onion Powder
Garlic Powder
Minced Garlic
Roasted Pimento Peppers (Drained)

Cooking Instructions

In a medium or large stock pot add 10 cups of chicken broth & 4 cups of water

Add 1 tbsp of chicken base

Bring soup liquid to a rolling boil

Reduce heat to med-low temp

Add 1 cup of each of mirepoix + (1) bunch of cut green onion

Add 1 cup of diced green bell pepper

Add vegetables of choice- 1 1/2 cup of each

Add dry seasoning (season to taste)

Add 1 cup of roasted pimento peppers

Add 1 tsp of minced garlic

Stir all ingredients well and let cook for 20-25 mins at med-lo temp

Add water as needed

Seafood Gumbo

Recipe Serves 6-8 servings

INGREDIENTS

Peeled & Deveined Shrimp
Diced Beef Stew Meat (Pre-cook)
1/8" Sliced Smoked Sausage (Pre-cook)
Sliced Patton's Hot Sausage Links (Pre-cook)
Blue Shell Crab Parts (Pre-sauteed in butter)
Parsley
Gumbo File
Salt
Black Pepper
Tony Chachere's Creole Seasoning
Onion Powder
Garlic Powder
Minced Garlic

Flour
Vegetable Oil
Chopped Yellow Onion
Chopped Celery
Chopped Bell Pepper
Chopped Green Onion
Bay Leaves

Cooking Instructions

In a medium non-stick saucepan or skillet
Add 1 cup of vegetable oil
Slowly add 3/4 cup of all-purpose flour and stir to mix flour into oil to make roux
Whisk oil and flour together constantly stirring
Cook roux at a med-low temp until fudge brown coloring
Don't let roux burn (PLEASE JESUS!!!.. You'll have to start over)
Add chopped yellow onion, celery, green onion, green/red bell pepper seasoning (1/4 cup of each)
Let roux cook with chopped seasoning for 5-7 mins
Transfer roux to medium or large stock pot
Add 6 quarts of water (Add water as needed)
Cook at high temp to allow roux to expand and bring to a boil
Keep stirring until roux expands and breaks and reduce heat to med-high temp
Add Tony Chachere's + dry seasoning (season to taste); Add 2 Bay Leaves
Add 2 lbs of each meat (Proteins) and let cook for 15-20 mins
Add 1 tbsp of gumbo file or Sassafras and stir in well
Add 2lbs shrimp & sauteed blue shell crab parts and let cook for 15-20 mins
(Skim/Remove excessive grease from top of Gumbo)
Serve with par-boiled white rice (Zataran's Brand)- Follow Directions

(For Best Results pre-cook/drain grease from all meats before adding to Gumbo)

***Do not over cook Gumbo as it may spoil because it contains seafood and other protein meat**

CHAPTER TWO

In this chapter we will cover 5 popular pasta dishes that are easy to make and will make your family love you forever maybe... if you don't mess it up.

- Zydeco Pasta
- Spagholive Pasta
- Beef Stroganoff
- Crawfish Monica Pasta
- Chicken or Shrimp Pasta

Zydeco Pasta
Recipe Serves 6-8 servings

INGREDIENTS

Peeled & Deveined Shrimp

Patton's Hot Sausage Links (Pre-cook)

Quarter Diced Chicken Breast

Parsley

Green Onion

Salt

Black Pepper

Tony Chachere's Creole Seasoning

Zataran's Seafood Boil

Shrimp Base

Zesty Sundried Tomatoes

Roasted & Diced Pimento Peppers

Heavy Whipping Cream

Corn Starch

Penne Pasta

Cooking Instructions

In a medium or large pot add 4 cups of water to boil penne pasta

Allow water to come to a rolling boil

Add tsp of oil & salt to taste

Add 1lb of penne pasta shells and cook for 8-10 mins

Cook and strain (Keep Pasta lightly oiled & moist)

In a large non-stick saucepan or skillet add 1/4 cup of vegetable oil and heat

Rinse & drain shrimp and chicken

Saute 2lbs of shrimp, hot sausage, diced chicken breast- med-hi for 7mins

Dice chicken breast after you've sauteed in nickel size pieces

Add 1/2 cup of zesty sun-dried tomatoes do not let burn

Drain excessive grease or liquid and set ingredients aside

In a medium or large pot add 2 1/2 quarts of heavy whipping cream and heat

Constantly stir with whisk to keep from burning

In a separate bowl add 1/4 cup of corn starch with 1/2 cup of water and whisk

Once cream gets hot add corn starch to thicken (Add additional starch as needed)

Add dry seasoning (season to taste)

Add 1 tbsp of chicken & seafood Base

Add sauteed shrimp, diced chicken, hot sausage, sun-dried tomatoes mix to cream base and stir

Add 1 (CAP) of Zataran's seafood boil to cream and stir thoroughly

Add 1 cup of cut green onion and stir all ingredients and cook for 5 mins

Add additional season if needed to cream base mix

In a large mixing bowl add penne pasta and 3 oz ladle of cream base mix per serving

Mix well and serve in pasta bowl

Spagholive Pasta

Recipe Serves 6-8 servings

INGREDIENTS:

Mayonnaise
Parsley
Salt
Pepper
Garlic Powder
Onion Powder
Spaghetti Pasta
Manzanilla Pitted Olives
Distilled White Vinegar

Cooking Instructions

In a medium or large pot add 4 cups of water to boil spaghetti pasta
Allow water to come to a rolling boil
Add 1 tbsp oil & 1 tsp of salt (to taste)
Add 1 lb spaghetti pasta No.3 (break pasta into half) and cook for 8-10 minutes
Cook and strain (Keep Pasta lightly oiled & moist)

In a medium mixing bowl
Add 4 cups of mayonnaise
Add cooked spaghetti pasta
Add 1 cup of manzanilla olives
Add dry seasoning (season to taste)
Add 2 tbsp of olive juice to pasta Mix
Add 1 tsp of white vinegar
Mix pasta and mayonnaise mixture until well blended and pasta is a creamy texture

Beef Stroganoff

Recipe Serves 6-8 servings

INGREDIENTS:

Diced Beef Stew Meat
Parsley
Green Onion
Salt
McCormick Beef Meat Seasoning
Beef Base
Sliced Baby Portabello Mushrooms
Heavy Whipping Cream
Corn Starch
Smetana
Egg Noodles Pasta

Cooking Instructions

In a medium or large pot add 4 cups water to boil egg noodle pasta
Allow water to come to a rolling boil
Add 2 tsp of oil & salt to taste
Add 1lb of egg noodle pasta and cook for 8-10 mins
Cook and strain (Keep Pasta lightly oiled & moist)

In a medium non-stick saucepan or skillet
Add 1/4 cup of 80/20 oil to fill bottom of pan or skillet and allow to heat at med-hi temp
Clean & drain beef stew meat
Saute diced beef stew meat with McCormick's Beef Meat seasoning for 15 mins or 85% cooked
Saute 1 cup of baby portabello mushrooms for 5 mins

In a medium or large pot add 2 quarts of heavy whipping cream and heat
Occasionally stir with whisk to keep from burning
In a separate bowl add 1/4 cup of corn starch with 3/4 cup of water and mix
Once cream gets hot add corn starch to thicken (Add additional starch as needed)
Add 1 tbsp of beef base and mix well
Add dry seasoning (season to taste)
Add 1/4 cup of worcestershire sauce and whisk thoroughly
Add 1 tsp of minced garlic and stir
Add diced beef stew meat & mushrooms to cream base and stir thoroughly with spoon
Add additional seasoning if needed to cream base mix

To Serve: add pasta on bottom and add Stroganoff on top with Smetana topping

Crawfish Monica Pasta

Recipe Serves 6-8 servings

INGREDIENTS:

Crawfish Tails
Large or Jumbo Shrimp- Peeled & Deveined
Parsley
Green Onion
Salt
Tony Chachere's Cajun Seasoning
Zataran's Crawfish Boil
Roasted & Diced Pimento Peppers
Corn Starch
Heavy Whipping Cream
Rotini Pasta

Cooking Instructions

In a medium or large pot add water to boil rotini pasta
Allow water to come to a rolling boil
Add 1 tsp of oil & salt to taste
Add 1lb of rotini pasta noodles
Cook and strain (Keep Pasta lightly oiled & moist)

In a medium non-stick saucepan or skillet
Add 80/20 oil to fill bottom of pan or skillet and let get hot at med-hi temp
Saute shrimp and crawfish tails with Tony Chachere's until 65% cooked or 7-10 minutes

In a medium or large pot add 3 quarts of heavy whipping cream and heat at med-low
Occasionally stir with whisk to keep from burning
In a separate bowl add 1/4 cup of corn starch with 3/4 cup of water
Once cream gets hot add corn starch to thicken (Add additional starch as needed)
Add sauteed shrimp & crawfish tails to cream base and stir thoroughly with cooking spoon
Add Tony Chachere's Cajun Seasoning (season to taste)
Add additional dry seasoning (season to taste)
Add 1 cup of cut green onions
Add 1 (CAP) of Crawfish Liquid Boil to mix and stir thoroughly

In a large mixing bowl add Rotini Pasta and cream base mix as needed and toss
Mix well and serve in pasta bowl

Chicken or Shrimp Pasta

Recipe Serves 6-8 servings

INGREDIENTS:

Diced Chicken Breast
Large or Jumbo Shrimp- Peeled & Deveined
Parsley
Green Onion
Salt
Tony Chachere's Cajun Seasoning
Zataran's Crawfish Boil
Roasted & Diced Pimento Peppers
Corn Starch
Heavy Whipping Cream
Penne Pasta

Cooking Instructions

In a medium or large pot add water to boil penne pasta
Allow water to come to a rolling boil
Add 1 tsp of oil & salt to taste
Add 1lb of penne pasta
Cook and strain (Keep Pasta lightly oiled & moist)

In a medium non-stick saucepan or skillet
Add 80/20 oil to fill bottom of pan or skillet and let get hot at med-hi temp
Saute shrimp or chicken with Tony Chachere's until 65% cooked or 7-10 minutes
Drain any excessive grease
(You may also substitute with Grilled Chicken Breast for added flavor)

In a medium or large pot add 3 quarts of heavy whipping cream and heat at med-low temp
Occasionally stir with whisk to keep from burning
In a separate bowl add 1/4 cup of corn starch with 3/4 cup of water
Once cream gets hot add corn starch to thicken (Add additional starch as needed)
Add 1/4 tbsp of chicken base for chicken pasta or shrimp base for shrimp pasta and mix
Add sauteed chicken or shrimp to cream base and stir thoroughly with cooking spoon
Add Tony Chachere's Cajun Seasoning (season to taste)
Add additional dry season (season to taste)
Add 1 cup of cut green onion
Add 1 (CAP) of Crawfish Liquid Boil to mix and stir thoroughly

In a medium mixing bowl add Penne Pasta and 3 oz of cream base mix per serving
Mix well and serve in pasta bowl

CHAPTER THREE

In this chapter we will cover 5 popular desserts that are easy to make and will make your family love you forever maybe... if you don't mess it up.

- New Orleans Bread Pudding
- Pear & Oatmeal Crisp
- Peach Cobbler
- Strawberries & Cream
- Banana Pudding

New Orleans Bread Pudding
Recipe Serves 6-8 Servings

INGREDIENTS:

Torn White Bread Loaf
Heavy Whipping Cream
Corn Starch
Condensed Milk
McCormick's Cinnamon Sugar

Raisins
Brown Sugar
Roasted Walnuts or Pecans
Jamaican Rum

Cooking Instructions

In a large mixing bowl add torn bread parts (2 Large Loafs of Regular White Bread)

Add 1 can of Condensed Milk & 1 1/2 quarts heavy whipping cream (4 quarts needed)

Add 1 cup of cinnamon sugar

Add 1 cup of brown sugar

Add 3 cups of Raisins

Add 2 cups of chopped Walnuts or Pecans (Make sure to keep some to add on top of pudding)

Mix all ingredients well and taste for flavor. Bread Pudding mix should have balanced sweet taste

BAKING:

In a 9x13 inch baking pan or dish use butter spray non-stick spray on the bottom to avoid sticking

Add Bread Pudding Mix and spread evenly in pan with spatula or cake spatula

Sprinkle Raisins, Walnuts or Pecans on top of Bread Pudding to garnish off

Preheat oven to 350 degrees

Cook Bread Pudding for 15-20 mins at 350 degrees uncovered and rotate

Continue to allow bread pudding to bake for another 10-15 minutes

Check Bread Pudding constantly to make sure it's baking evenly and not burning

You may reduce heat to 300 degrees to allow Bread Pudding to bake evenly

Check to see if Bread Pudding has hardened by inserting a toothpick in the center. If there is no food residue on toothpick remove Bread Pudding from oven and let cool down. If there is residue on toothpick allow Bread Pudding to bake until all moisture or wetness has baked and has been absorbed by heat.

Vanilla Rum Sauce Directions:

In a medium or large pot add 2 1/2 quarts of Heavy Whipping Cream

In a separate bowl add 1/4 cup of corn starch with 3/4 cup of water

Once cream gets hot add corn starch to thicken (Add additional starch as needed)

Add 2 tbsp of Pure Vanilla Extract

Add 1 cup of Jamaican Rum and drink some straight from the bottle for good luck!

Add 2 cups of Cinnamon Sugar & Brown Sugar

Whisk all ingredients well and heat at med-low heat for 5-7 minutes or until creamy smooth

Pear & Oatmeal Crisp

Recipe Serves 6-8 Servings

INGREDIENTS:

Sliced Pears
Oatmeal
Baking Powder
McCormick's Cinnamon Sugar
Brown Sugar

Cooking Instructions

Drain canned pears and use 6 cups of pears
Use a 9x13 inch baking pan or baking dish

Add 1 1/2 cup of oatmeal in mixing bowl
Add 1/2 cup of cinnamon sugar
Add 1/2 cup of brown sugar
Add 1 tbsp of baking powder
Add 3/4 cup of melted butter or margarine to oatmeal mix to make crumbled oatmeal pieces
Mix oatmeal mixture thoroughly

BAKING:
Add oatmeal crumbles to canned pears in baking pan or dish
Cover entire pan of pears with oatmeal pieces to bake

Preheat oven to 400 degrees
Cover pear crisp with aluminum foil to bake in oven
Allow pear crisp to bake 25 minutes covered
Rotate pear crisp and keep covered for additional 20-25 minutes
Remove aluminum foil from pear crisp and let bake for 15-18 minutes uncovered @ 300 degrees
Check pear crisp to make sure no burning or scorching is taking place (Reduce Heat if necessary)
Bake pear crisp until golden brown and crispy crust topping
Allow to cool and serve

(THIS RECIPE IS ALSO GOOD FOR APPLE & PEACH CRISP)

Peach Cobbler
Recipe Serves 6-8 Servings

Ingredients:

Canned Peaches
Pie Dough
McCormick's Cinnamon Sugar
Brown Sugar
Corn Starch
Sweetened Condensed Milk

Cooking Instructions

Drain canned Peaches but keep the liquid. use 6 cups of peaches
In a 9x13 inch baking dish or baking pan spray non-stick pan spray on the bottom
Lay dough crust sheet on bottom of pan filling entire pan; shape dough crust to fit bottom & top of pan
Add drained peaches on top of dough crust and spread
In a medium pot add peach juice and 1 cup of water and heat
In a separate bowl add 1/4 cup of corn starch with 3/4 cup of water
Once pear juice gets hot add corn starch to thicken (Add additional starch as needed)
Add 1/2 cup of brown sugar to liquid cobbler filling
Add cobbler filling to peaches in baking pan and spread evenly
Add top layer of dough crust sheet on top of cobbler and sprinkle brown sugar and cinnamon on top

BAKING:

Preheat oven to 400 degrees

Cover peach cobbler with aluminum foil to bake in oven
Allow peach cobbler to bake 15 minutes covered
Rotate peach cobbler and keep covered for additional 10-15 minutes
Remove aluminum foil from pear crisp and let bake for 10-15 minutes uncovered
Check peach cobbler to make sure no burning or scorching is taking place (Reduce Heat if necessary)
Bake peach cobbler until golden brown and crispy crust
Allow to cool and serve

Peach Cobbler goes well with Homemade Vanilla Ice Cream and Whipped Cream Topping

(THIS RECIPE IS ALSO GOOD FOR APPLE COBBLER)

Strawberries & Cream

Recipe Serves 6-8 servings

INGREDIENTS:

Strawberries- 2 flats
Condensed Sweetened Milk- 2 cans
Homogenized Milk- 1/2 gallon

Cooking Instructions

Rinse and clean strawberries (You can cut Strawberries in half to increase portion size)

Allow strawberries to drain

In a serving bowl add 2 cans of Condensed Sweetened Milk

Add 1/2 gallon of Homogenized Milk of choice

Whisk all ingredients together thoroughly

Add Strawberries and chill to 35 degrees

Serve in small bowls

Banana Pudding
Recipe Serves 6-8 servings

Ingredients:

Ripe Bananas
Jumbo Eggs
Homogenized Whole Milk- 1/2 gallon
Vanilla Extract
Vanilla Wafers
All Purpose Flour
Sugar

Cooking Instructions

Crack eggs and separate the yolks from the whites of the egg and set aside the whites.
In a small non-stick skillet or saucepan
Add 2 1/2 cups of homogenized whole milk
Add 1/2 cup sugar
Add 3 tbsp of flour and 1/2 tsp salt
Stir in the 3 egg yolks
Add 1 tbsp of vanilla extract and whisk all ingredients well to make creamy pudding mix
Heat at medium heat uncovered and whisk ingredients until pudding mixture thickens
Remove from heat and let cool

BAKING:
In a 9x13 inch baking dish or baking pan
Arrange a layer of vanilla wafers on the bottom of pan
Spread pudding mix on top of vanilla wafers
Add sliced bananas crosswise about 1/8 inch thick on top of Wafers and pudding
Repeat this process to make layers of pudding ending with vanilla wafers on top

Meringue Topping:
Preheat Oven to 400 degrees
Beat or mix egg whites at high speed with a pinch of salt until stiff
Gradually beat in the remaining 1/4 cup sugar and continue beating until you can't beat them anymore
Spread the meringue over the pudding with a spatula
Making a few decorative mountain peaks with meringue on top of banana pudding
Bake or use brulee torch to lightly brown-off meringue topping

Thank You from Author

I wanted to take this opportunity to thank some very special people in my life because without them this book would not be possible. First and foremost I want to thank my master and creator. God, I love and thank you for each and every blessing and gift you've entrusted with me. I may not always get it right but you know I won't stop until I get it right. Thank you for your hand of protection, guidance and grace. You are always at the head of my life and your mercy has allowed me to make it this far.

To my wonderful mother Belinda Johnson. There are no words to describe the amount of love and respect I have for you. You have been there for me every step of the way and have helped me to accomplish and achieve so much in my life and career. You are God's greatest gift to me. Your sacrifices and covering has allowed me to make it this far.
Mom I love you!

To my beautiful grandmother Joyce DeJean. It all started for me being with you in your kitchen watching you prepare our family Sunday dinners every week. You allowed me to harass you, get in your way, ask questions, argue with you, challenge you and aggravate your nerves every weekend I spent with you. I grew up in your kitchen and little did I know you were grooming me to become who I am today and to be able to offer many of our family's recipes for the world to know and love. You have supported me and encouraged me from the very beginning. Thank you for pouring into me and building me to be a culinary professional and understanding the power and importance of a "Home Cooked Meal"! You are my heart.

To my family, know that I love you all! Too many of you to name but you all are the bomb.com

To many of my colleagues in the industry who I've worked with or have admired from afar. Please know that you have played an intricate part to my culinary career and success. To my friend Chef Arthur Thomas, Chef Ben Davis, Rachel Ray, Chef Gordon Ramsay, Chef Emeril Lagasse, Chef G. Garvin, Patti Labelle, Chef Paul Lewis, Joshua Hairgrove and many others who I cannot name I say "Thank You".

To all of my supporters and clients that I have had the privilege of serving over my culinary career I say "Thank You"! More importantly thank you for entrusting me to prepare meals from my heart and soul for you to enjoy. To my Houston Café Inc Restaurant & Catering Services staff, Pioneer Culinary Solutions staff and certainly my Soulful Chef staff, "THANK YOU"!

I pray these recipes will help bring your family back together and put enjoyment back into being in the kitchen. A family that cooks together can't complain that nobody doesn't cook for them!! (Smile)